SCALING DOWN

By Trudie Hughes

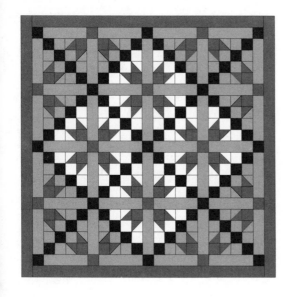

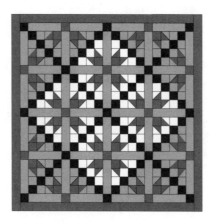

Patterns and Techniques for 11 Small
Scale Quilts, a Feathered Star Setting
and 12 Pieced Borders

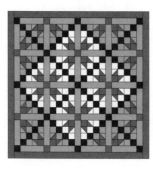

Acknowledgments

I would like to thank all the technical people at LaserMaster, Corel, and Word Perfect for their help in seeing me through this manuscript.

A special thanks to Inge Dick, my personal sewing slave. She organized me, cheered me and cleaned up after me, so this book would be possible.

Credits:

Photography	Bill Lemke
Editing and Nit-picking	Darlene Hays
Illustrations	Trudie Hughes

This book was produced on a Compaq 386 with Ventura, Corel Draw and Word Perfect.

Scaling Down©
©1990 by Trudie Hughes
PW Publications
13330 Watertown Plank Road
Elm Grove, WI 53122

Printed in the United States of America

Table of Contents

Introduction

This book is an extension of the techniques and patterns presented in my *Template-Free™ Quiltmaking* books. Although this time we will explore working in a smaller scale, the basic techniques remain the same. Because of the size of the pieces, however, good sewing skills will be even more important. Some of the patterns have been changed to make the piecing easier, too.

The quilts presented in this book are all quite challenging, but worth the effort. They may be bordered as desired and finished as a small quilt, or set into a large feathered star that uses an 18" center.

This book is divided into four sections:

1. In the beginning of the book, I have provided a tips section that will discuss specific techniques that are critical to small scale quiltmaking. It is assumed that you have had some experience with the rotary cutter and the sewing machine.

2. The next section contains 11 small quilt patterns, all designed to finish to 18" square.

3. After the quilt patterns, directions are given to make a large feathered star quilt, using an 18" small scale quilt as the center.

4. The last section of the book provides 12 pieced border plans to make your feathered star quilt even more impressive. All are figured to fit the 38" feathered star and you can mix and match as you choose.

The *Template-Free™* books are published by That Patchwork Place, P.O. Box 118, Bothell, WA 98041.

TIPS FOR SMALL SCALE QUILTS

Since all the math of my quiltmaking is based on adding a ¼" seam allowance to all pattern pieces, I did not want to change just because I wanted to work with smaller pieces. That is why these are small scale quilts and not miniature. This way, you can cut and piece these quilts with the techniques you have been using.

However, there are some tips that will make the job easier. You will also have to be much more careful with the cutting and piecing, since there is very little forgiveness in these smaller pieces.

SEAM ALLOWANCE

Sewing the correct seam allowance is even more important in these smaller quilts. You want to sew a seam that will result in things turning out to be the right size. I highly suggest trying my sewing test to find out if you are on the right track before you start.

In machine piecing we press the seams to one side. You will find that you will lose some measurement in the seam allowance. Although we add a ¼" seam allowance to the pieces in the cutting, YOU DO NOT SEW A REAL ¼" SEAM. ¼ " is too large. The seams are really "scant" ¼" seams. The sewing test will help you find where you need to watch when you sew. You may be able to off-set your needle, or use masking tape as a guide.

SEWING TEST

Take 3 strips about 4" long and 1¼" wide. Sew them side by side. Press. Measure from raw edge to raw edge. This piece should now be 2¾" wide. You will find you may have to lighten up your sewing or things will begin to shrink quickly.

I have tried to remind you what units should measure whenever possible. That way you can find when you are off, before you get into too much trouble.

SEWING STRIPS

When the directions require you to sew strips before sub-cutting, cut all strips in half first (approx. 22" long). It will be easier to handle these skinny strips and you will have much less distortion when you press.

LINING UP PIECES

Care must be taken to line up pieces at the beginning and end of seams along the edge you are actually going to sew. If you feel they shift at your machine, pin, or use the point of your seam ripper to hold them in place as you sew.

I find it best to actually lift your presser foot and place it down on pieces as you sew, rather than to just push them up under the presser foot.

Slow down when going over seams. Some machines deviate from the seam allowance at bumps. If you are really cautious and slow at these important areas, accuracy will increase.

MINIATURE TRIANGLES

There are some techniques that work best for small quilts, and one is making half-square triangles by the bias method that I introduced in my first book, *Template-Free Quiltmaking* and also used in the Feathered Star quilt in my book *Even More.*

To make these triangles, you start by adding ¾" to the finished size of the triangle needed. This measurement is the width to cut the bias strips. In this book, the triangles finish to ¾". Therefore, we will be cutting 1½" wide bias strips.

The miniature triangles will be made from ¼ yd. pieces. From this size piece, you can get 80 finished triangle units. If you need less of these, use fat eighths (cut your ¼ yd. piece in half).

Place the two fabrics that will make up the triangles right sides together. Place the 45° angle that is on the Rotary Rule™ on the selvage and cut. Using this cut edge as a guide, cut pairs of strips 1½" wide.

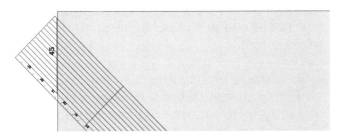

Sew these pairs of strips together and press while in pairs, being careful not to stretch them. Press right side up. Then, sew 3 sets of pairs. I like to use 4 pairs, but if this is a new technique for you, start by trying 3 pairs first.

Place the 45° angle on a stitching line and cut. This places you back on grain. Make cuts at 1¼" (the finished size of the triangle plus its ½" seam). It will be well worth your time to check the 45° angle frequently. Do this by sliding the ruler over fully onto the stitching line and seeing if you continue to cut at 45° angles.

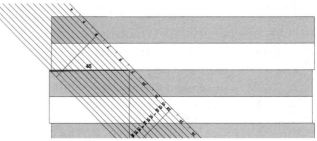

With these strips, place the cross line of the Rotary Mate ™ on the long cut edge and cut at each point.

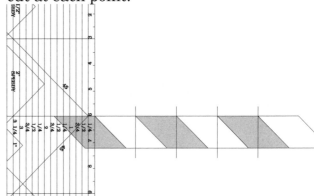

Then line up the ruler with the cross line and 1¼" marking and clean these up to perfect 1¼" squares. Now we have tiny triangle units that are already pressed.

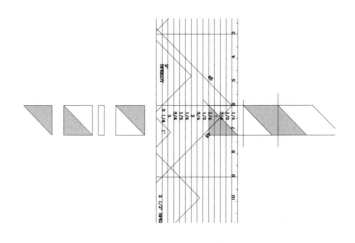

RULERS

It is necessary to cut as accurately as possible. My rulers, the Rotary Rule ™ and the Rotary Mate™, are designed for the techniques used in these patterns.

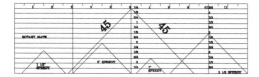

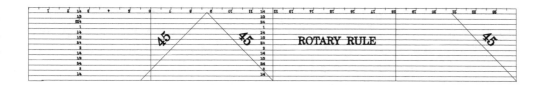

These rulers are available from:

Patched Works, Inc.
13330 Watertown Plank Road
Elm Grove, Wisconsin 53122

FINISHING

The quilts in this book have been machine quilted. I find that the smaller the quilt, the thinner the batting should be. You do not want to distort all the intricate piecing.

The bindings were cut 2" wide on straight grain, single layer. Then they were mitered to make nice square corners. You can bind these quilts with any method you are most comfortable, however.

Review Section:

HOW TO CUT TRAPEZOIDS

These shapes start with strips. Some designs will have you work with strips all right sides up and some will have you work with strips folded in half. Be sure to read instructions carefully.

Working with four layers at a time, cut left edge perpendicular with the top and bottom edges. From the left edge, measure the distance called for in the pattern and make a dot at the top edge, unless the pattern tells you otherwise.

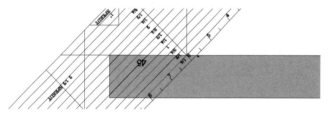

Cut with the 45° mark on the ruler lined up with the longer cut edge and stop just short of the dot.

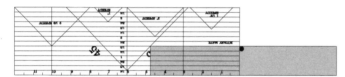

The next cut does not have to be marked. From the new point, measure the desired amount and make a straight cut.

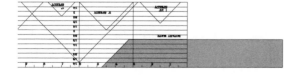

HOW TO CUT "DECAPITATED TRI-ANGLES"

Although this shape is really a trapezoid, I refer to it as a "decapitated triangle" to help you form a mental picture of the shape you will need to cut. These shapes remind me of a quarter-square triangle with its tip cut off.

Cut the required width strip. Using the Rotary Mate™, align the 45° angle marking with the top edge of strip. Cut.

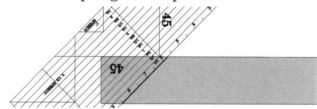

Measure along edge of strip until you get to desired length and make a dot.

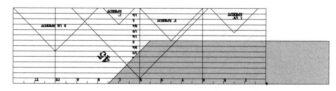

Line up ruler with dot and cut a 45° angle in the opposite direction.

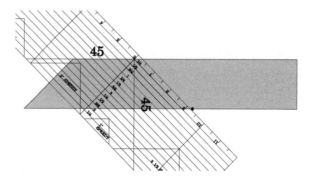

ROAD TO OKLAHOMA

Color photos on pages 44 and 52

A ☐   B ☐   C ☐   D ☐

Fabric Requirements:

Fabric A (Light Background)- ⅜ yd.
Fabric B (Medium Background) - ⅔ yd.
Fabric C (Chain) -¼ yd.
Fabric D (Stars) - ⅜ yd.
Border - ¼ yd.
Binding - ¼ yd.
Backing - ⅔ yd.

Pieced area finishes to 15¾".

If you are making this to set into a feathered star, see page 58 for additional yardage required.

Cutting Instructions

Fabric A (Light Background)

1. Cut and set aside a 9" by 22" piece.

2. Cut 2 strips 1¼" wide. Cut in half. From one of these, cut 16 squares 1¼".

Fabric B (Medium Background)

1. Cut and set aside a 9" by 22" piece.

2. Cut 2 strips 1¼" wide. Cut in half. From one of these, cut 16 squares 1¼".

3. Cut 2 strips 3½" wide. Cut every 1¼" to yield 40 rectangles 3½" by 1¼".

Fabric C (Dark Fabric for Chain)

1. Cut 3 strips 1¼" wide. Cut in half. With one of these, cut 13 squares 1¼".

Fabric D (Accent Fabric for Stars)

1. Cut and set aside 2 pieces 9" by 22".
2. Cut 2 strips 1¼" wide. Cut into 44 squares 1¼".

Piecing and Assembly

1. Place 9" by 22" piece of accent fabric (D) right sides together with piece of light background (A) and cut into 1½" wide bias strips.

To make these bias triangles, refer to page 6.

You will need 32 triangles that look like this:

2. Do the same with the other Fabric D piece and the Fabric B piece. You will need 32 triangles that look like this:

3. With strips of Fabric C, Fabric B and Fabric A, make two each of the following sets of strips:

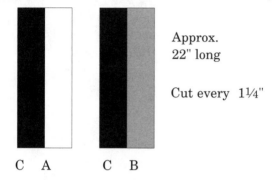

C A   C B

Approx. 22" long

Cut every 1¼"

4. Make 8 four-patches that look like this:

Make 8 four-patches that look like this:

Make 16 four-patches that look like this:

5. Make 4 blocks that look like this:

These should measure 3½" by 3½" raw edge to raw edge.

Make 4 blocks that look like this:

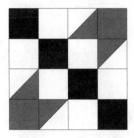

These should measure 3½" by 3½" raw edge to raw edge.

Make 8 blocks that look like this:

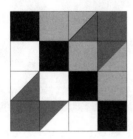

These should measure 3½" by 3½" raw edge to raw edge.

6. Following illustration, assemble blocks with lattice strips.

7. If you are making this to set into a feathered star, add 1⅝" wide strips of border fabric to build this quilt to 18".

8. If you are finishing this as a small quilt, add borders as desired.

JACOB'S ELEVATOR

Color photos on pages 48 and 50

A ☐   B ▨   C ▪   D ▪

Fabric Requirements:

Fabric A (Background) - ¼ yd.
Fabric B (Bright) - ¼ yd.
Fabric C (Large Print) - ¼ yd.
Fabric D (Accent) - ¼ yd.
Border - ¼ yd.
Binding - ¼ yd.
Backing - ⅔ yd.

Pieced area finishes to 15".

If you are making this to set into a feathered star, see page 58 for additional yardage required.

Cutting Instructions

Fabric A (Light)

1. Cut 2 strips 1¼" wide for four-patches and puss-in-the-corner blocks. Cut in half.

2. Cut 1 strip 2" wide for puss-in-the-corner blocks. Cut in half.

3. Cut 1 strip 2⅜" wide. Cut into 10 squares 2⅜". Cut these diagonally to yield 20 half-square triangles for square-in-square blocks.

Fabric B (Bright)

1. Cut 2 strips 2⅜" wide. Cut into 24 squares 2⅜". Cut these diagonally to yield 48 half-square triangles for flying geese units.

Fabric C (Large Print)

1. Cut 1 strip 4¼" wide. Cut into 6 squares 4¼". Cut these squares with an X to yield 24 quarter-square triangles for flying geese units.

2. Cut 1 strip 2⅝" wide. Cut into 5 squares 2⅝" for square-in- square blocks.

Fabric D (Accent)

1. Cut 2 strips 1¼" wide for four patches and puss-in-the-corner blocks. Cut in half.
2. Cut 1 strip 2" wide for puss-in-the-corner blocks. Cut in half.

Piecing and Assembly

1. With the 1 1/4" strips, make 2 sets of strips that look like this:

Approx. 22" long

D A

Place these strips right sides together and cut every 1¼".

Sew pairs together to make 16 four-patches.

These should measure 2" raw edge to raw edge.

2. Make 24 Flying Geese units.

These should measure 2" by 3½" raw edge to raw edge.

See pg. 19 for more information on piecing these units.

3. Make one strip that looks like this:

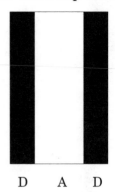

Approx. 22" long

D   A   D

Make 8 cuts at 1¼".

Make one strip that looks like this:

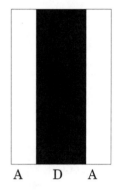

Approx. 22" long

A   D   A

Make 4 cuts at 2".

Make 4 puss-in-the-corner blocks.

These should measure 3½" raw edge to raw edge.

4. Make 5 square-in-square blocks.

These should measure 3½" raw edge to raw edge.

5. This quilt is pieced in rows across the quilt. There are wide rows and narrow rows. Follow illustration to assemble quilt.

6. If you are making this to set into a feathered star, add 2" wide strips of border fabric to build quilt to 18".

7. If you are finishing this as a small quilt, add borders as desired.

SAWTOOTH FLOWER

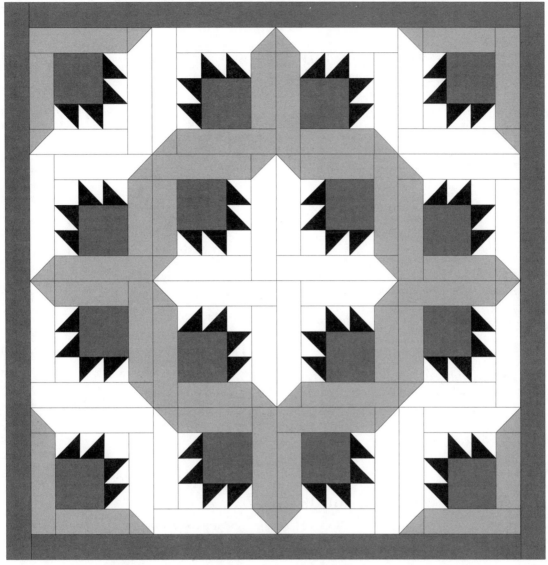

Color photos on pages 46 and 50

A ☐　B ▨　C ▨　D ▨

Fabric Requirements:

Fabric A (Background) - ½ yd.
Fabric B (Main) - ¼ yd.
Fabric C (Accent) - ¼ yd.
Fabric D (Stems) - ⅓ yd.
Border - ¼ yd.
Binding - ¼ yd.
Backing - ⅔ yd.

Pieced area finishes to 15".

If you are making this to set into a feathered star, see page 58 for additional yardage required.

Cutting Instructions

Fabric A (Background)

1. Cut 2 strips 1¼" wide. With both strips right sides up, cut 16 trapezoids at 3⅞" intervals, beginning measurement along **top** edge. (See pg. 8 for more information on cutting these.)

These trapezoids should look like this:

2. Cut 2 strips 1¼" wide. With both strips right sides up, cut 16 trapezoids at 4⅝" intervals, beginning measurement along **bottom** edge (See pg. 8 for more information on cutting these.)

These trapezoids should look like this:

3. Cut 1 strip 1¼" wide. Cut into 16 squares 1¼".

4. Set aside ¼ yd. to be sewn with Fabric C (accent) to make bias triangles.

Fabric B (Main)

1. Cut 1 strip 2" wide. Cut into 16 squares 2".

Fabric C (Accent)

1. Set aside ¼ yd. to be sewn with Fabric A (background) for bias triangles.

Fabric D (Stems)

1. Cut 1 strip 2¾" wide. Cut into 16 rectangles 1¼" by 2¾".

2. Cut 1 strip 3½" wide. Cut into 16 rectangles 1¼" by 3½" .

3. Cut 1 strip 1⅝" wide. Cut into 16 squares 1⅝". Cut these diagonally to yield 32 half-square triangles.

Piecing and Assembly

1. Place the ¼ yd. of Fabric A (background) right sides together with Fabric C (accent) and cut into 1½" wide bias strips.

To make these bias triangles, refer to page 6.

These triangles will measure 1¼" raw edge to raw edge. You will need 64 of these units.

2. Sew 16 triangle pairs going in one direction.

Sew these to the Fabric B squares.

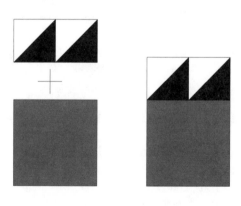

3. Sew 16 pairs going the other direction. Add a background square and add to center block:

  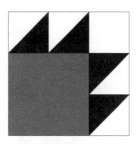

4. Add the 2¾" and 3½" strips of stem fabric to block:

5. Sew triangle of Fabric D (stem) to end of trapezoids and add to block:

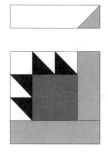 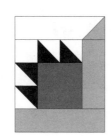 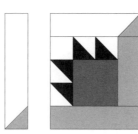 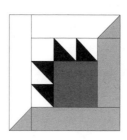

These blocks should measure 4¼" raw edge to raw edge. Make 16 blocks.

6. Sew blocks together following illustration.

7. If you are making this to set into a feathered star, add 2" wide strips of border fabric to build quilt up to 18".

8. If you are finishing this as a small quilt, add borders as desired.

ROAD TO ST. LOUIS

Color photos on pages 42 and 51

A [ ] B [■]

Fabric Requirements:

Fabric A (Background) - ⅓ yd.
Fabric B (Main) - ¼ yd.
Assorted Scraps - 128 squares 1½"
Border - ¼ yd.
Binding - ¼ yd.
Backing - ⅔ yd.

Pieced area finishes to 16".

If you are making this to set into a feathered star, see page 58 for additional yardage required.

Cutting Instructions

Fabric A (Background)

1. Cut 1 strip 5¼" wide. Cut into 2 squares 5¼". Cut these with an X to yield 8 quarter-square triangles.

2. Cut 1 strip 2⅞" wide. Cut into 8 squares 2⅞". Cut these diagonally to yield 16 half-square triangles.

Fabric B (Main)

1. Cut 1 strip 5¼" wide. Cut into 4 squares 5¼". Cut these with an X to yield 16 quarter-square triangles.

Piecing and Assembly

1. Make 8 flying geese units that finish to look like this:

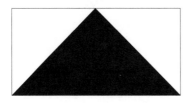

HINT:

When piecing these, set first triangle in corner and sew.

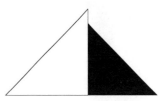

When second triangle is added, set in corner, but be sure that the seams intersect at ¼".

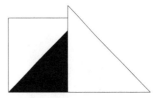

Results should be a straight edge, leaving a ¼" seam allowance.

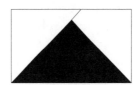

These should measure 2½" by 4½" raw edge to raw edge.

2. Make 4 quarter-square triangle units that look like this:

3. Make 5 sixteen-patches of scraps that look like this:

These should measure 4½" by 4½" raw edge to raw edge.

4. Make 4 half-blocks of scraps that look like this:

These should measure 4½" by 2½" raw edge to raw edge.

5. Make 4 four-patches of scraps that look like this:

These should measure 2½" by 2½" raw edge to raw edge.

6. Assemble quilt in rows following illustration.

7. If you are making this to set into a feathered star, add 1½" wide strips of border fabric to build quilt up to 18".

8. If you are finishing this as a small quilt, add borders as desired.

JUDY'S STAR

Color photos on pages 45 and 51

A ☐   B ▨   C ■

Fabric Requirements:

Fabric A (Background) - ½ yd.
Fabric B (Main) - ¼ yd.
Fabric C (Accent) - ¼ yd.
Border - ¼ yd.
Binding - ¼ yd.
Backing - ⅔ yd.

Pieced area finishes to 17".

If you are making this to set into a feathered star, see page 58 for additional yardage required.

Cutting Instructions

Fabric A (Background)

1. Cut 1 strip 5½" wide. Cut into 4 squares 5½". Cut these squares with an X to yield 16 setting triangles.

2. Cut 3 strips 1½" wide. Cut into 64 squares 1½".

3. Cut 1 strip 2¼"wide. Cut into 16 squares 2¼". Cut these with an X to yield 64 quarter- square triangles.

4. Cut 1 strip 3½" wide. Cut into 8 squares 3½".

Fabric B (Main)

1. Cut 1 strip 2¼" wide. Cut into 16 squares 2¼". Cut these with an X to yield 64 quarter- square triangles.

2. Cut 1 strip 1½" wide. Cut into 16 squares 1½" for centers of stars.

Fabric C (Accent)

1. Cut 2 strips 1⅞" wide. Cut into 32 squares 1⅞". Cut these diagonally to yield 64 half-square triangles.

Piecing and Assembly

1. With Fabric A (background) on top of Fabric B (main), sew the short sides of the quarter-square triangles in pairs like this:

When opened, all will look like this:

2. Add a half-square triangle of Fabric C (accent).

3. Assemble 16 blocks that look like this:

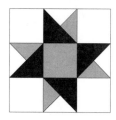

These should measure 3½" raw edge to raw edge.

4. Piece the blocks in rows starting in a corner, following illustration. Since this is a diagonally set quilt, take care in joining rows and add corners last.

5. If you are making this to put into a feathered star, add 1" strips of border fabric to build quilt to 18".

6. If you are finishing this as a small quilt, add borders as desired.

EVENING IN IRELAND

Color photos on pages 40 and 49

A ☐   B ◼   C ▢

Fabric Requirements:

Fabric A (Background) - ½ yd.
Fabric B (Double chain) - ½ yd.
Fabric C (Single chain) - ⅓ yd.
Border - ¼ yd.
Binding - ¼ yd.
Backing - ⅔ yd.

Pieced area finishes to 16½".

If you are making this to set into a feathered star, see page 58 for additional yardage required.

Cutting Instructions

Fabric A (Background)

1. Cut 1 strip 3½" wide for puss-in-the-corner blocks. Cut into 12 rectangles 2¾" by 3½".

2. Cut 1 strip 2" wide for the puss-in the corner blocks. Cut in half.

3. Cut 2 strips 1¼" wide for the 5-patch blocks. Cut in half.

4. Cut 1 strip 2¾" wide. Cut into 9 squares 2¾". Cut these with an X to yield 36 quarter- square triangles.

Fabric B (Double chain)

1. Cut 4 strips 1¼" wide for 5-patch blocks. Cut in half.

2. Cut 2 strips 1¼" wide for the puss-in-the-corner blocks. Cut in half.

3. Cut 2 strips 1⅝" wide. Cut into 36 squares 1⅝". Cut diagonally to yield 72 half-square triangles.

Fabric C (Single chain)

1. Cut 1 strip 2" wide. Cut into 9 squares 2".

2. Cut 2 strips 1¼" wide. Cut into 36 squares 1¼".

3. Cut 3 strips 1¼" wide for the 5-patch blocks. Cut in half.

Piecing and Assembly

This small quilt is made up of three blocks.

EVENING STAR BLOCKS

1. Make 36 flying geese units that finish to look like this:

These should measure 1¼" by 2" raw edge to raw edge. Refer to page 19.

2. This star is pieced in three rows:

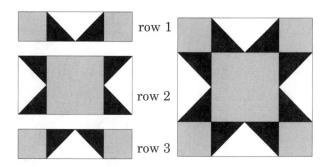

Make 9 blocks.

When the star block is completed, it should measure 3½" square, raw edge to raw edge.

PUSS- IN -THE- CORNER BLOCK

1. Make 2 sets of strips that look like this:

Approx. 22" long

Cut every 1¼"
Make 24 cuts

B   A   B

2. Sew one of these units onto each side of large rectangle.

Make 12 puss- in -the- corner blocks.

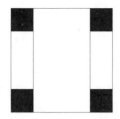

These blocks should measure 4¼" by 3½" raw edge to raw edge.

FIVE-PATCH BLOCKS

1. Make one of each set of strips that look like this:

T h e s e   Strips are approx. 22" long

Row 1   Row 2   Row 3

C B A B C   B C B C B   A B C B A

strips should measure 4¼" raw edge to raw edge.

2. Place row 1 and row 2 right sides together and cut every 1¼". Sew together in 8 pairs.

Take row 3 and make 4 cuts at 1¼". Sew between 2 pairs of rows 1 and 2.

Make 4 blocks that look like this:

These blocks should measure 4¼" square raw edge to raw edge.

Assemble quilt in rows following illustration.

If you are making this to set into a feathered star, add 1¼" wide strips of border fabric to build quilt up to 18".

If you are finishing this as a small quilt, add borders as desired.

SHORTCUT TO SCHOOL

Color photos on pages 41 and 52

A ▭   B ▭   C ▭   D ▭

Fabric Requirements:

Fabric A (Background) -⅓ yd.
Fabric B (Main) - ⅓ yd.
Fabric C (Accent) - ¼ yd.
Fabric D (Accent) - ¼ yd.
Border - ¼ yd.
Binding - ¼ yd.
Backing - ⅔ yd.

Pieced area finishes to 16".

If you are making this to set into a feathered star, see page 58 for additional yardage required.

Cutting Instructions

Fabric A (Background)

1. Cut 3 strips 1½" wide. With strips folded in half, right sides together, cut trapezoids, measuring cuts at 2⅜" intervals.

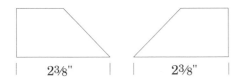

| 2⅜" | | 2⅜" |

You will need 32 trapezoids with points going in one direction and 32 trapezoids with points going in the opposite direction.

(See page 8 for more information on cutting these.)

2. Cut 2 strips 1½" wide. Cut 4 "decapitated triangles" cutting back at 8¼", and cut 8 "decapitated triangles" cutting back at 5¾".

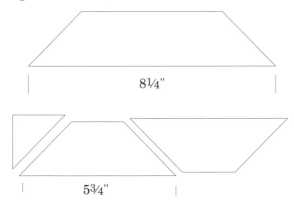

| 8¼" |

| 5¾" |

(See page 8 for more information on cutting these.)

Fabric B (Main)

1. Cut 2 strips 1⅞" wide. Cut into 32 squares 1⅞". Cut these squares diagonally to yield 64 half-square triangles.

2. Cut 3 strips 1" wide for nine-patches. Cut these in half.

3. Cut 1 strip 3¼" wide. Cut this into 2 squares 3¼". Cut these squares with an X to yield 8 quarter-square triangles.

Fabric C (Accent)

1. Cut 2 strips 1½" wide for large four-patches. Cut in half.

2. Cut 2 strips 1" wide for the nine-patches. Cut in half.

Fabric D (Accent)

1. Cut 2 strips 1½" wide for large four-patches. Cut in half.

2. Cut 2 strips 1" wide for the nine-patches. Cut in half.

Piecing and Assembly

1. With 1" strips, make one of each of the following sets of strips. Strips are 22" long.

D   B   D   C   B   C

Press all seams towards fabric B.

These strips should measure 2" wide when pressed. Make 16 cuts at 1".

Make 1 each of the following sets of strips:

Approx. 22" long

B   D   B   B   C   B

Press seams towards B.

Make 8 cuts at 1".

Make 8 nine-patches of each combination.

2.   Make 2 sets of strips for larger four-patches that look like this:

Approx. 22" long

D   C

Place these strips right sides together and make 9 cuts at 1½". Sew these pairs to make four- patches that look like this:

3.   From leftovers of previous step, cut every 1½" to make 12 units that look like this:

You will need 2 loose 1½" squares of each accent fabric for the corners of the quilt.

4.   Sew a half-square triangle (B) to each trapezoid (A).

HINT:

Press seams towards triangles on trapezoids with points going to the upper right.

Press seams towards trapezoids when the points are going to the upper left.

This will be helpful when sewing two trapezoids together, as seams will be going opposite directions.

5. Assemble quilt in rows following illustration.

6. The first border is made up of "decapitated triangles" (A) and quarter-square triangles (B).

Make 4 border strips that look like this:

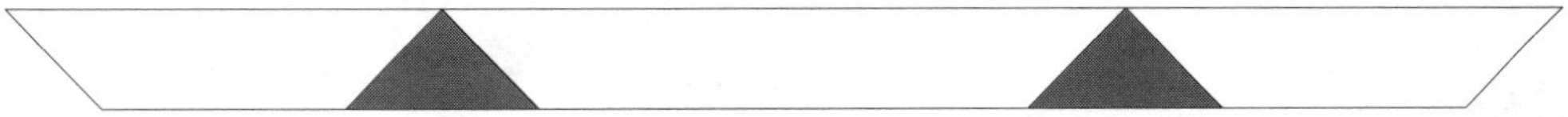

When adding these to the quilt, begin and end backstitching ¼" from the ends, then miter out.

7. If you are making this to set into a feathered star, add 1½" wide strips of border fabric to build quilt up to 18".

8. If you are finishing this as a small quilt, add borders as desired.

CHIMNEYS AND CORNERSTONES

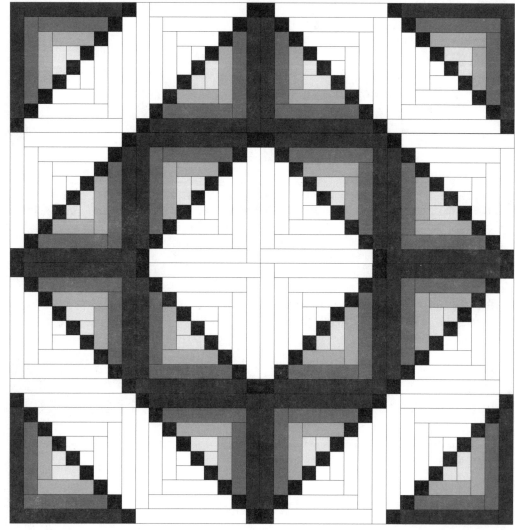

Color photos on pages 37 and 51

A ☐   B ■   C ☐   D ☐   E ☐   F ■

Fabric Requirements:

Fabric A (Background) - ½ yd.
Fabric B (Accent) - ¼ yd.
Fabric C (First Dark) - ¼ yd.
Fabric D (Second Dark) - ¼ yd.
Fabric E (Third Dark) - ¼ yd.
Fabric F (Fourth Dark) - ⅜ yd.
Border - ¼ yd.
Binding - ¼ yd.

Pieced area finishes to 18".

If you are making this to set into a
feathered star, see page 58 for additional
yardage required.

Cutting Instructions

Fabric A (Background)

1. Cut the ½ yd. piece in half along the fold. Cutting along the 22" length, cut one each of the following width strips :

1", 1½", 2", 2½", 3", 3½", 4", 4½"

Fabric B (Accent)

1. Cut 5 strips 1" wide. Cut in half.

Fabric C (First Dark)

1. Cut 1 strip 1" wide. Cut in half.
2. Cut 1 strip 1½" wide. Cut in half.

Fabric D (Second Dark)

1. Cut 1 strip 2" wide. Cut in half.
2. Cut 1 strip 2½" wide. Cut in half.

Fabric E (Third Dark)

1. Cut 1 strip 3" wide. Cut in half.
2. Cut 1 strip 3½" wide. Cut in half.

Fabric E (Fourth Dark)

1. Cut 1 strip 4" wide. Cut in half.
2. Cut 1 strip 4½" wide. Cut in half.

Piecing and Assembly

1. Sew a Fabric B (accent) strip onto the 1" wide background strip and to all the dark strips. Press all seams towards the accent strips. Stack and cut every 1". You will need 16 cuts from each for the quilt.

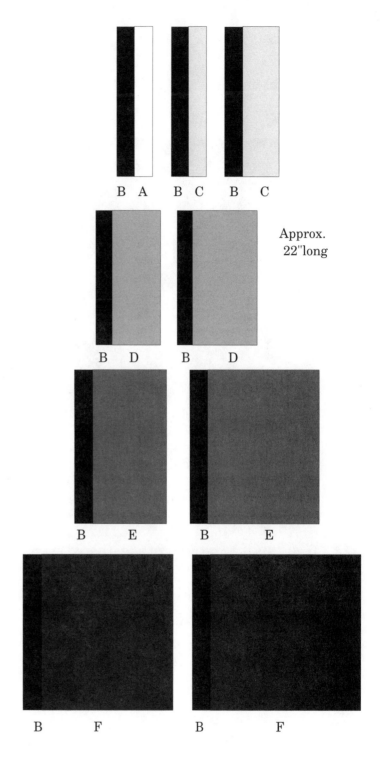

2. Stack the background strips and cut every 1". You will need 16 cuts for the quilt.

3. Working from the center out, assemble 16 log cabin blocks that look like this:

NOTE:

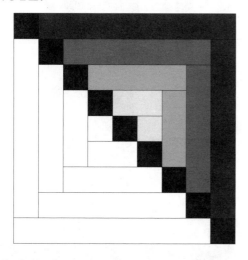

When adding light strips, press seams towards center. When adding dark strips, press seams towards outside of block. That way, seams will be going opposite directions at accent intersections.

4. Following illustration, assemble quilt in rows.

5. If this is to be used in a feathered star, no border is necessary.

6. If you are finishing this as a small quilt, add borders as desired.

FLYING GEESE IN THE CABIN

Color photos on pages 43 and 50

A ⬜ B ⬛ C ▨ D ▨ E ⬛

Fabric Requirements:

Fabric A (Background) - ½ yd.
Fabric B (Accent) -¼ yd.
Fabric C (First Dark) - ¼ yd.
Fabric D (Second Dark) - ½ yd.
Fabric E (Third Dark) - ⅓ yd.
Border -¼ yd.
Binding - ¼ yd.
Backing -⅔ yd.

Pieced area finishes to 16".

If you are making this to set into a feathered star, see page 58 for additional yardage required.

Cutting Instructions

Fabric A (Background)

1. Take the ½ yd. piece and cut in half along the fold. Cutting along the 22" length, cut one of each of the following width strips:

1½", 2", 2½", 3", 3½", 4"

Fabric B (Accent)

1. Cut 1 strip 1½" wide. Cut into 16 squares 1½".

2. Cut 3 strips 1⅞" wide. Cut into 48 squares 1⅞". Cut diagonally to yield 96 half-square triangles.

Fabric C (First Dark)

1. Cut 1 strip 2" and 1 strip 2½" wide.

Fabric D (Second Dark)

1. Cut 1 strip 3" and 1 strip 3½" wide.

Fabric E (Third Dark)

1. Cut 1 strip 4" and 1 strip 4½" wide.

Piecing and Assembly

1. From each of the Fabric A (background) strips, make 16 cuts at 1".

2. From each of the dark strips, make 16 cuts at 1".

3. Each round is assembled as a regular log cabin. Care needs to be taken that all strips begin and end matched. This will ensure that all blocks will be square and will all measure the same.

Each round will use 2 light strips and 2 dark strips. Then, using the Rotary Mate™, line up the two 45° angles (the V feature) at the intersection and cut two opposite corners off (between the dark and light).

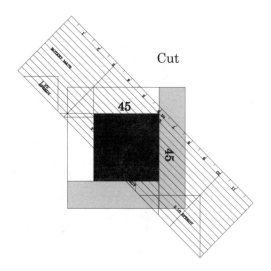

Cut

Add a triangle onto these corners. This is done to each round of light and dark.

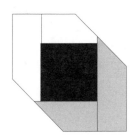 

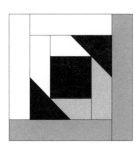 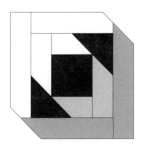

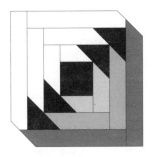

4. Make 16 blocks that look like this:

5. Assemble quilt in rows, following llustration.

6. If you are making this to set into a feathered star, add 1½" wide border strips to build the quilt to 18".

7. If you are finishing this as a small quilt, add borders as desired.

This quilt pattern was first written for *More Tempate-Free Quiltmaking*, but cut and pieced entirely differently. This is a much easier way of piecing this design.

Even though this is a book about small scale quilts, I am including information to make it in a lap size and a full size quilt, too.

Lap Quilt

Pieced area finishes to 40" by 60"
After first border, quilt will be 44" by 64"
After last border, quilt will be 50" by 70"

Fabric Requirements:

Fabric A (Background) - 1¼ yds.
Fabric B (Accent) - 1½ yds. (1 yd. for piecing, ½ yd. for first border)
Fabric C (First dark) - ¼ yd.
Fabric D (Second Dark) - ⅜ yd.
Fabric E (Third Dark) - ½ yd.
Fabric F (Fourth Dark) - ⅝ yd.
Last border - ¾ yd.
Binding - ¾ yd.
Backing - 3½ yds.

Cutting Instructions

Fabric A (Background)

1. Cut one of each of the following width strips:

1½", 2½", 3½", 4½", 5½", 6½", 7½", 8½".

Fabric B (Accent)

1. Cut 2 strips 2½" wide into 24 squares 2½" for block centers.

2. Cut 8 strips 2⅞" wide into 96 squares 2⅞". Cut these diagonally to yield 192 half square triangles.

3. Cut 6 strips 2½" wide for first border.

Fabric C (First Dark)

Cut 1 strip 2½" and 1 strip 3½" wide.

Fabric D (Second Dark)

Cut 1 strip 4½" and 1 strip 5½" wide.

Fabric E (Third Dark)

Cut 1 strip 6½" and 1 strip 7½" wide.

Fabric F (Fourth Dark)

Cut 1 strip 8½" and 1 strip 9½" wide.

Last Border

Cut 7 strips 3½" wide.

Piecing and Assembly

1. From all strips of Fabric A and Fabrics C, D, E, and F, make 24 cuts at 1½". Assemble 24 blocks following the instructions for the small quilt. You will have 4 rounds. These blocks finish to 10½".

2. The lap quilt is set four blocks across and six down.

3. Add borders.

Large Quilt

The large quilt uses 48 blocks and is set 6 blocks across and 8 blocks down. Double the yardage and cut twice the number of pieces of the lap quilt.

Chimneys and Cornerstones by Trudie Hughes, Elm Grove, Wisconsin,
 1990, 48" square.
Pattern found on page 30.
This quilt uses Border #12.

Snowball by Trudie Hughes, Elm Grove, Wisconsin, 1990. 52" square.
Pattern found on page 53.
This quilt uses Border #5.

County Line by Trudie Hughes, Elm Grove, Wisconsin, 1990, 54" square.
Pattern found on page 56.
This quilt uses Border # 11.

Evening in Ireland by Trudie Hughes, Elm Grove, Wisconsin, 1990, 52" square.
Pattern found on page 23.
This quilt uses Border #2.

Shortcut to School by Trudie Hughes, Elm Grove, Wisconsin, 1990, 55" square.
Pattern found on page 26.
This quilt uses Border #7.

Road to St. Louis by Trudie Hughes, Elm Grove, Wisconsin, 1990, 50" square.
Pattern found on page 18.
This quilt uses Border #10.

Flying Geese in the Cabin by Trudie Hughes, Elm Grove, Wisconsin, 1990, 55" square.
Pattern found on page 33.
This quilt uses Border #4.

Road to Oklahoma by Trudie Hughes, Elm Grove, Wisconsin, 1990, 50" square.
Pattern found on page 9.
This quilt uses Border #3.

Judy's Star by Trudie Hughes, Elm Grove, Wisconsin, 1990, 54" square.
 Pattern found on page 21.
This quilt uses Border # 6.

Sawtooth Flower by Trudie Hughes, Elm Grove, Wisconsin, 1990, 55" square.
Pattern found on page 15.
This quilt uses Border #8.

Album Quilt by Trudie Hughes, Elm Grove, Wisconsin, 1990, 51" square.
This small quilt design can be found in the book *More Template-Free™ Quiltmaking*
by Trudie Hughes.
This quilt uses Border #9.

Jacob's Elevator by Trudie Hughes, Elm Grove, Wisconsin, 1990, 54" square.
Pattern found on page 12.
This quilt uses Border #1.

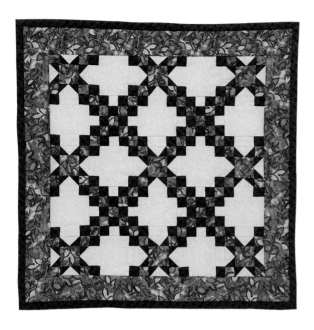

Evening In Ireland by Trudie Hughes,
Elm Grove, Wisconsin, 1990.
Pattern found on page 23.

Snowball by Trudie Hughes,
Elm Grove, Wisconsin, 1990.
Pattern found on page 53.

County Line by Trudie Hughes, Elm Grove,
Wisconsin, 1990.
Pattern found on page 56.

Flying Geese in the Cabin by Trudie
Hughes, Elm Grove, Wisconsin, 1990.
Pattern found on page 33.

Sawtooth Flower by Trudie Hughes,
Elm Grove, Wisconsin, 1990.
Pattern found on page 15.

Jacob's Elevator by Trudie Hughes,
Elm Grove, Wisconsin, 1990.
Pattern found on page 12.

Chimneys and Cornerstones by
Trudie Hughes, Elm Grove,
Wisconsin, 1990.
 Pattern found on page 30.

Road to St. Louis by Trudie Hughes,
Elm Grove, Wisconsin, 1990.
Pattern found on page 18.

Judy's Star by Trudie Hughes,
Elm Grove, Wisconsin, 1990.
Pattern found on page 21.

Road to Oklahoma by Trudie Hughes,
Elm Grove, Wisconsin, 1990.
Pattern found on page 9.

Shortcut to School by
Trudie Hughes, Elm Grove,
Wisconsin, 1990.
Pattern found on page 26.

Snowball

Color photos on pages 38 and 49

A B C

Pieced area finishes to 17"

Fabric Requirements:

Fabric A (Background) -½ yd.
Fabric B (Main) - ⅓ yd.
Fabric C (Accent) -¼ yd.
Border -¼ yd.
Binding -¼ yd.
Backing -⅔ yd.

If you are making this to set into a feathered star, see page 58 for additional yardage required.

Cutting Instructions

Fabric A (Background)

1. Cut 2 strips 3½" wide. Cut into 16 squares 3½". Using the 1" Speedy on the Rotary Mate ™ ruler, cut 2 corners off each of 4 squares, 3 corners off each of 8 squares, and all 4 corners off each of 4 squares to make the snowball blocks.

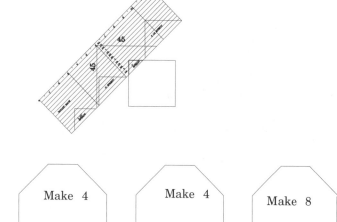

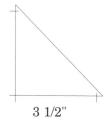

Make 4   Make 4   Make 8

2. Cut 1 strip 5½" wide. Cut into 3 squares 5½". Cut these with an X to yield 12 quarter-square triangles.

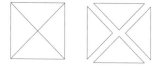

It would be helpful to notch these triangles at 3½".

3 1/2"

Fabric B (Main)

1. Cut 2 strips 1½" wide. Cut these in half.

2. Cut 2 strips 1⅞" wide. Cut into 24 squares 1⅞". Cut these in half diagonally to yield 48 half-square triangles. It would be helpful to nub these at 1½".

3. Cut 2 squares 3" in half diagonally to yield 4 half-square triangles for the corners.

Fabric C (Accent)

1. Cut 3 strips 1½" wide. Cut these in half.

Piecing and Assembly

1. Make 1 each of the following sets of strips:

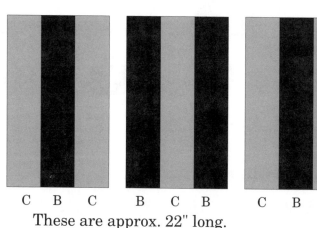

C B C   B C B   C B C

These are approx. 22" long.

Place rows 1 and 2 right sides together and make 9 cuts at 1½". Sew in pairs.

With row 3, make 9 cuts at 1½". Add these to the pairs to make 9 nine-patches that look like this:

These should measure 3½" raw edge to raw edge.

2. Add a Fabric B triangle onto all the corners of the snowball blocks.

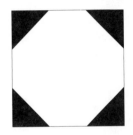  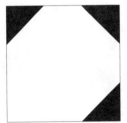

3. Assemble quilt in rows starting in a corner. Add corners last.

4. If you are making this to set into a feathered star, add 1" wide border strips to build quilt up to 18".

5. If you are finishing this as a small quilt, add borders as desired.

COUNTY LINE

Color photos on pages 39 and 49

A ▢ B ▢ C ▢ D ▢ E ▢

Fabric Requirements:

¼ yd. each of 5 fabrics. This quilt is most dramatic when shaded light to dark.
Border - ¼ yd.
Binding - ¼ yd.
Backing - ⅔ yd.

Pieced area finishes to 15".

If you are making this to set into a feathered star, see page 58 for additional yardage required.

Cutting Instructions

Fabric A (Very light)

1. Cut 3 strips 1¼" wide. Cut in half.

Fabric B (Light)

1. Cut 3 strips 1¼" wide. Cut in half.

Fabric C (Medium)

1. Cut 2 strips 1¼" wide. Cut in half.
2. Cut 1 strip 2" wide. Cut in half.

Fabric D (Dark)

1. Cut 1 strip 1¼" wide. Cut in half.
2. Cut 1 strip 2¾" wide. Cut in half.

Fabric E (Darkest)

1. Cut 1 strip 1¼" wide. Cut in half.
2. Cut 1 strip 3½" wide. Cut in half.

Piecing and Assembly

1. Make 1 each of the following sets of strips:

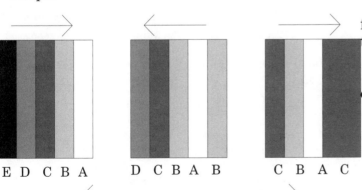

E D C B A   D C B A B   C B A C

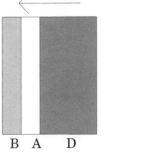

Strips are approx. 22"long

B   A   D   A   E

Arrows indicate direction to press seams.

These each should measure 4¼" wide, raw edge to raw edge.

2. Off each strip, make 16 cuts at 1¼". Sew into 5 rows to yield a block that looks like this:

Row 1
Row 2
Row 3
Row 4
Row 5

Press seams towards row 1.

Make 16 blocks. These blocks should measure 4¼" by 4¼", raw edge to raw edge.

3. Assemble quilt following illustration.

4. If you are making this to set into a feathered star, add 2" wide border strips to build quilt to 18".

5. If you are finishing this as a small quilt, add borders as desired.

FEATHERED STAR

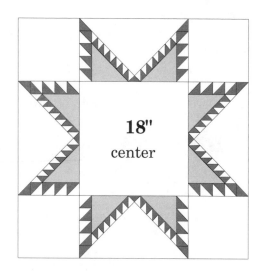

This feathered star is a perfect showcase for your 18" small scale quilts. It is a great setting for any of the quilts in this book or any other small pieced or appliqued blocks you may want to frame. See color photos on pages 37-48.

Pieced area finishes to 38" square

Fabric Requirements:

This yardage includes fabric used in the feathered star and the pieced border.

Add these yardages to the fabric requirements given for the small scale quilts.

Fabric A (Background)- 2½ yds. (1¾ yds. for piecing, ¾ yd. for pieced border)
Fabric B (Accent Fabric)- 1¼ yds. (¾ yd. for piecing, ½ yd. for pieced border)
Fabric C (Main Fabric) - 2¼ yds. (¼ yd. for piecing, ¾ yd. for pieced border,   1¼ yds. for first and last borders)
Binding - ½ yd.
Backing- 3½ yds.

CUTTING INSTRUCTIONS

Fabric A (Background)

1. Cut 2 strips 10½" wide. Cut into 4 squares 10½".

2. Cut 1 square 19¼". Cut with an X to yield 4 quarter-square triangles.

3. Cut 1 strip 2⁵⁄₁₆" wide. Cut into 4 squares 2⁵⁄₁₆". Cut these diagonally to yield 8 half-square triangles.

4. Set aside ½ yd. to make triangles with Fabric B (accent).

Fabric B (Accent)

1. Set aside ½ yd. to go with Fabric A (background) for bias strips .

2.   Cut 4 squares 2⅞". Cut these diagonally to yield 8 half-square triangles for the feather points.

3.   Cut 2 squares 2⁵⁄₁₆".   Cut these diagonally to yield 4 half-square triangles.

Fabric C (Main)

1. Cut 1 strip 6⅞" wide. Cut into 4 squares 6⅞". Cut these diagonally to yield 8 half-square triangles.

Binding

1. Cut 6 strips 2½" wide for binding.

Piecing and Assembly

There are many ways of making triangle units. Choose the one you are most comfortable with.

You need 32 large triangles and 48 small triangles.

2½"   1¹⁵⁄₁₆"

The larger triangle units should measure 2½" from raw edge to raw edge; the smaller triangles should measure 1¹⁵⁄₁₆" from raw edge to raw edge.

Bias Method

For more detailed information on this technique, see page 6.

1. With Fabric A (background) and Fabric B (accent fabric) right sides together, cut 6 bias strips 2" wide and 6 bias strips 2½" wide.

2. You will be making two different sets of sewn strips, the 2" strips for the small triangles and the 2½" strips for the larger triangles. Sew into pairs:

Three at a time is easiest.

Press gently and join pairs, press again.

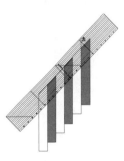

3. Lining up the 45° line that is in the middle of the Rotary Rule™ on one of the stitching lines, make bias cuts at 2½" for the larger triangles and 1¹⁵⁄₁₆" for the smaller triangles. (This is just halfway between 1⅞" and 2".) This will put the strips back on grain.

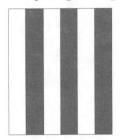

Be sure to make 45° cuts. Check frequently by sliding ruler all the way onto the strips to see if cuts are still at 45°.

4. Line up the crossline on the ruler with the cut edge and cut at all the points along the top.

5. Now measure off 2½" for the larger triangles and 1¹⁵⁄₁₆" for the smaller triangles.

This cut should hit the next point.

6. Sew 6 smaller triangle units together. Sew 4 strips going one direction

and 4 strips going the other direction.

These strips should measure 9" from raw edge to raw edge.

Add a small Fabric A (background) triangle to the end of each strip to look like this:

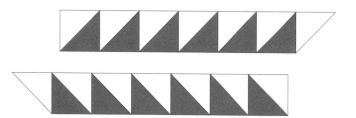

Sew these to long side of large triangles.

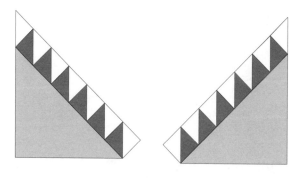

7. Sew 4 larger triangle units together. Sew 4 strips heading one direction.

Sew 4 strips going the opposite direction.

These strips should measure 8½" from raw edge to raw edge.

Following illustration, add large triangle strips to short sides of larger triangles.

Make 4 that look like this:

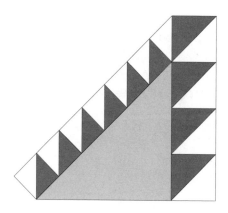

and 4 that look like this:

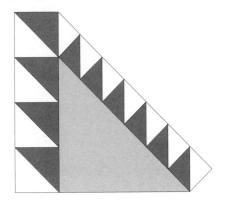

8. Sew a Fabric B (accent) 2⅞" triangle to the ends.

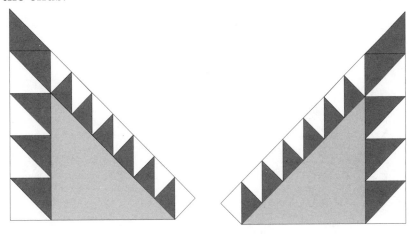

9. Add one of these triangle units to large background triangle. Add a small triangle to the other triangle unit; join to Fabric A (background) triangle.

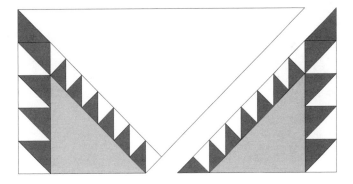

10. Sew one of these units to each side of
the pieced center section.

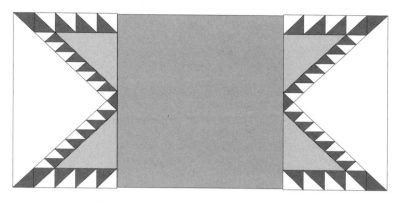

11. Onto each side of the remaining two
units, sew a Fabric A (background) square:

12. Sew these three rows together.

13. After pieced area
is completed, add
borders.

Pieced Borders

The pieced borders presented here use only two or three fabrics: a background fabric, the main fabric and usually an accent fabric.

In order for the pieced borders to fit the feathered star, a first border of a specific measurement is required. This border could be broken into two borders if you wish, but you can not change the total size needed.

There are 12 borders for you to choose from.

1 Color photo on page 48	**2** Color photo on page 40	**3** Color photo on page 44
4 Color photo on page 43	**5** Color photo on page 38	**6** Color photo on page 45
7 Color photo on page 41	**8** Color photo on page 46	**9** Color photo on page 47
10 Color photo on page 42	**11** Color photo on page 39	**12** Color photo on page 37

Border 1

After star is completed, add the first border.

With 2½" wide strips of border fabric, cut 2 strips 38½" long and sew to 2 opposite sides. Press.

Cut 2 strips 42½" long and sew to remaining sides. Press.

Fabric Requirements:

Fabric A (Background) - ⅓ yd.
Fabric B (Main) - ½ yd.
Fabric C (Accent) - ⅓ yd.

Cutting Requirements

Fabric A (Background)

1. Cut 2 strips 4¼" wide. Cut into 14 squares 4¼". Cut these with an X to yield 56 quarter-square triangles.

2. Cut 4 squares 3½ " from remaining.

Fabric B (Main)

1. Cut 3 strips 3⅞" wide. Cut into 28 squares 3⅞". Cut these diagonally to yield 56 half-square triangles.

Fabric C (Accent)

1. Cut 2 strips 4¼" wide. Cut into 14 squares 4¼". Cut these with an X to yield 56 quarter-square triangles.

Piecing and Assembly

1. With the quarter-square triangles of Fabrics A and C, sew 28 pairs that look like this:

And sew 28 pairs that look like this:

2. Sew all of these to a half-square triangle of Fabric B to make 56 units in all, going in two different directions.

3. For each side, sew 7 units going one way and 7 going the other way.   Sew two border strips to two opposite sides of quilt.

Sew a corner square of Fabric A onto two remaining border strips and add to quilt.

4. After the pieced border is applied, the quilt will measure 48" square.

5. Add a last border of any width desired.

Border 2

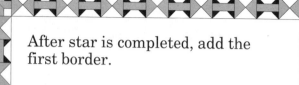

After star is completed, add the first border.

With 1" wide strips of border fabric, cut 2 strips 38½" long and sew to 2 opposite sides. Press.

Cut 2 strips 39½" long and sew to remaining sides. Press.

Fabric Requirements:

Fabric A (Background) - ⅝ yd.
Fabric B (Main) - ½ yd.
Fabric C (Accent) - ¼ yd.

Cutting Instructions

Fabric A (Background)

1. Cut 2 strips 4¼" wide. Cut into 14 squares 4¼". Cut these with an X to yield 56 quarter-square triangles.

2. Cut 5 strips 1½" wide. Cut 56 "decapitated triangles", cutting back at 4¼". (See pg. 8 for more information on cutting these.)

4 1/4"

3. Cut 4 squares 1½".

Fabric B (Main)

1. Cut 2 strips 4¼" wide. Cut into 14 squares 4¼". Cut these with an X to yield 56 quarter-square triangles.

2. Cut 1 strip 3½" wide. Make 24 cuts at 1½".

3. Cut 1 strip 1½" wide. With strips folded in half, cut 8 trapezoids, 4 with points going one way and 4 with the points going the other way, cutting back at 2⅞". (See pg. 8 for more information on cutting these.)

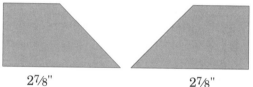

2⅞"   2⅞"   **F a b**

ric C (Accent)

1. Cut 3 strips 1⅞" wide. Cut into 52 squares 1⅞". Cut these diagonally to yield

104 half-square triangles.

Piecing and Assembly

1. Make 24 units that look like this:
2. Make 28 units that look like this:

3. Make 4 corner units that look like this:

4. Make 4 sets of border strips with 13 units, alternating the two types of units,

that look like this:
5. Sew two to opposite sides of quilt. To the remaining strips, add a corner unit and

add to quilt.
6. After the pieced border is applied, the quilt will measure 45" square.

7. Add a last border of any width desired.

Border 3

After star is completed, add first border.

With 1½" wide strips of border fabric, cut 2 strips 38½" long and sew to 2 opposite sides. Press.

Cut 2 strips 40½" long and sew to remaining sides. Press.

Fabric Requirements:

Fabric A (Background) - ½ yd.
Fabric B (Main) - ¼ yd.
Fabric C (Accent) - ¼ yd.

Cutting Instructions

Fabric A (Background)

1. Cut 1 strip 5¼" wide. Cut into 4 squares 5¼". Cut these with an X to yield 16 quarter-square triangles.

2. Cut 2 strips 2⅞" wide. Cut these into 26 squares 2⅞". Cut these diagonally to yield 52 half -square triangles.

Fabric B (Main)

1. Cut 1 strip 5¼" wide. Cut into 5 squares 5¼"". Cut these with an X to yield 20 quarter-square triangles.

Fabric C (Accent)

1. Cut 2 strips 2⅞" wide. Cut into 22 squares 2⅞". Cut these diagonally to yield 44 half-square triangles.

Piecing and Assembly

1. Sew flying geese units that measure 2½" by 4½" raw edge to raw edge.

Make 20 units that finish to look like this:

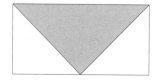

Press seams towards center.

Make 16 units that finish to look like this:

Press seams towards outside.

2. You will also need 12 corner units that look like this:

3. Make 4 border strips, with a triangle unit on each end, that look like this:

Sew two onto opposite sides of the quilt.

Add remaining corner squares to the other border strips and sew onto quilt.

4. After the pieced border is applied, the quilt will measure 44" square.

5. Add a last border of any width desired.

Border 4

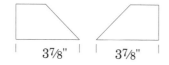

After star is completed, add first border.

With 1¾" wide strips of border fabric, cut 2 strips 38½" long and sew to 2 opposite sides. Press.

Cut 2 strips 41" long and sew to remaining sides. Press.

Fabric Requirements:

Fabric A (Background) - ⅔ yd.
Fabric B (Main) - ⅓ yd.
Fabric C (Accent) - ⅓ yd.

Cutting Instructions

Fabric A (Background)

1. Cut 4 strips 3½" wide. Cut into 64 rectangles 2" by 3½".

2. Cut 2 strips 2" wide. With strips folded in half, cut 16 trapezoids, cutting back at 3⅞". (See page 8 for more information on cutting these.)

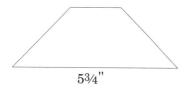

You will need 8 with points going one way and 8 with points going the other way.

3. Cut 1 strip 2" wide. Cut 4 "decapitated triangles", cutting back at 5¾". From the remainder of this strip, cut 4 squares 2".

Fabric B (Main)

1. Cut 2 strips 3⅜" wide. Cut into 21 squares 3⅜". Cut these with an X to yield 84 quarter-square triangles.

2. Cut 2 squares 1⅞". Cut these diagonally to yield 4 half-square triangles for corners.

Fabric C (Accent)

1. Cut 2 strips 3⅜" wide. Cut into 18 squares 3⅜". Cut these with an X to yield 72 quarter-square triangles.

2. Cut 1 strip 1⅞" wide into 6 squares 1⅞". Cut these diagonally to yield 12 half-square triangles.

Piecing and Assembly

1. With quarter-square triangles of fabrics B and C, make 32 A units that look like this:

Make 32 B units that look like this:

2. Make 4 center turning units that look like this:

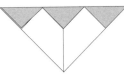

3. Make 4 of each of these border ends that look like this:

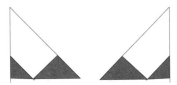

4. Make 4 corner units that look like this:

5. Onto one side of each center turning unit, attach 8 A units. Onto the other side of each center turning unit, attach 8 B units.

6. Add 2 border ends to each border strip. Add two border strips to opposite sides of quilt.

7. Add corners to both ends of remaining border strips.

Add these border strips to quilt.

8. After the pieced border is applied, the quilt will measure 46⅞" square.

9. Add a last border of any width desired.

Border 5

After star is completed, add first border.

With 1½" wide strips of border fabric, cut 2 strips 38½" long and sew to 2 opposite sides. Press.

Cut 2 strips 40½" long and sew to remaining sides. Press.

Fabric Requirements:

Fabric A (Background) - ¼ yd.
Fabric B (Main) - ½ yd.
Fabric C (Accent) - ½ yd.

Cutting Instructions

Fabric A (Background)

1. Cut 2 strips 1⅞" wide. Cut into 80 squares 1⅞ ". Cut these diagonally to yield 160 half-square triangles.

2. Cut 1 strip 1½" wide. Fold in half and cut into 8 trapezoids, measuring along cut edge at 3⅞" intervals.

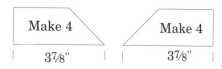

Make 4   Make 4
3⅞"   3⅞"

Fabric B

(Main)

1. Cut 8 strips 1½" wide. Fold strips in half and cut into 80 trapezoids, measuring along cut edge at 3⅞" intervals.

You will need 40 that look like this:

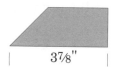

3⅞"

And 40 that look like this:

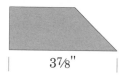

3⅞"

2. Cut 4 squares 2½" for corner units.

Fabric C (Accent)

1. Cut 8 strips 1 ½" wide. Fold strips in half and cut into 80 trapezoids, measuring along cut edge at 3⅞" intervals.

You will need 40 that look like this:

3⅞"

And 40 that look like this:

3⅞"

Piecing and Assembly

1. Sew a triangle onto the end of all Fabric B and C trapezoids. Press seams in opposite directions.

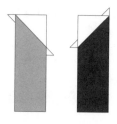

2. Make 40 A units that look like this:

3. Make 40 B units that look like this:

4. Make 4 corner units that look like this:

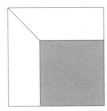

5. Sew 4 strips of 10 A units and 4 strips of 10 B units in a row. Join an A strip to a B strip. Sew two of these to opposite sides of quilt.

6. Add a corner unit to remaining strips and add these border strips to quilt.

7. After the pieced border is applied, the quilt will measure 46" square.

8. Add a last border of any width desired.

Border 6

After star is completed, add first border.

With 2½" wide strips of border fabric, cut 2 strips 38½" long and sew to 2 opposite sides. Press.

Cut 2 strips 42½" long and sew to remaining sides. Press.

Fabric Requirements:

Fabric A (Background) - ¾ yd.
Fabric B (Main) - ½ yd.
Fabric C (Accent) -½ yd.

Cutting Instructions

Fabric A (Background)

1. Cut 8 strips 2⅜" wide. Cut into 116 squares 2⅜". Cut these diagonally to yield 232 half-square triangles.

2. Cut 4 squares 2⅝" for corners.

Fabric B (Main)

1. Cut 6 strips 2" wide. With strips folded in half, cut into 64 diamonds.

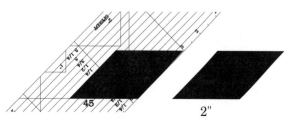

Fabric C (Accent)

1. Cut 5 strips 2" wide. Cut into 56 diamonds.

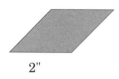

2"

Piecing and Assembly

1. Sew a triangle onto each bias edge of diamonds. Press seams towards triangles when adding to fabric B. Press seams towards diamond when adding to fabric C. By having these seam allowances going in opposite directions, intersections will match.

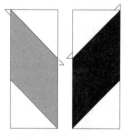

2. Make 28 A units that look like this:

3. Make 28 B units that look like this:

4. Make 4 corner units that look like this:

5. Sew 4 strips of 7 A units in a row and 4 strips of 7 B units in a row. Join an A unit to a B unit.

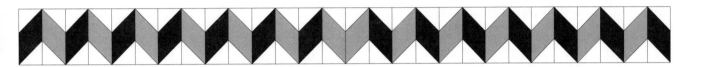

Sew two of these border strips to quilt.

6. Add a corner unit to ends of remaining border strips and add to quilt.

7. After the pieced border is applied, the quilt will measure 49¼" square.

8. Add a last border of any width desired.

Border 7

After star is completed, add the first border.

With 2¾" wide strips of border fabric, cut 2 strips 38½" long and sew to 2 opposite sides. Press.

Cut 2 strips 43" long and sew to remaining sides. Press.

Fabric Requirements:

Fabric A   (Background)- ⅔ yd.
Fabric B (Main) - ⅔ yd.
Fabric C (Accent) - ⅓ yd.

Cutting Instructions

Fabric A (Background)

1. Cut 4 strips 3⅜" wide. Cut into 44 squares 3⅜". Cut these with an X to yield 176 quarter-square triangles.

Fabric B (Main)

1. Cut 8 strips 2" wide.

Fabric C (Accent)

1. Cut 4 strips 2" wide.

Piecing and Assembly

1. Make 4 sets of strips that look like this:

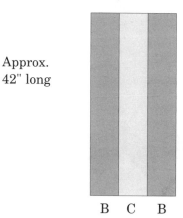

Approx. 42" long

Cut every 2"

B   C   B

Press all seams towards fabric B.

2.   Sew a quarter-square triangle onto the ends of 64 of these units.

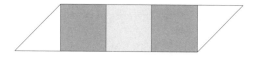

3. Make 4 fill- in units that look like this:

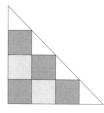

4.   Make 4 corner units that look like this:

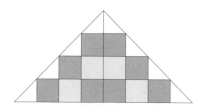

5. Make 4 border strips of 16 units:

6. Add a fill-in unit to the right end of each strip.

7. Sew one of these to each side of the quilt.

8. Add corner units to quilt.

9. After the pieced border is applied, the quilt will measure 49" square.

10. Add a last border of any width desired.

Border 8

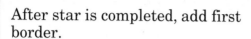

After star is completed, add first border.

With 3⅛" wide strips of border fabric, cut 2 strips 38½" long and sew to opposite sides. Press.

Cut 2 strips 43¾" long and sew to remaining sides. Press.

Fabric Requirements:

Fabric A (Background) - ½ yd.
Fabric B (Main) - ½ yd.
Fabric C (Accent) - ½ yd.

Cutting Instructions

Fabric A (Background)

1. Cut 2 strips 2⅝" wide. Cut into 28 squares 2⅝". Cut with an X to yield 112 quarter-square triangles.

2. Cut 3 strips 1½" wide. Cut one of these in half. From one of the half-strips, cut 4 rectangles 1½" by 2½".

3. Cut 2 squares 2¼". Cut these diagonally for the corner half-square triangles.

4. Cut 2 squares 4⅛". Cut these with an X to yield 8 quarter-square triangles for turning units.

Fabric B (Main)

1. Cut 4 strips 1½" wide. Cut one of these in half. From one of the long strips, cut 4 rectangles 1½" by 4½" and 8 squares 1½".

2. Cut 3 strips 2½" wide. Cut into 56 rectangles 1½" by 2½".

Fabric C (Accent)

1. Cut 7 strips 1½" wide. With strips folded in half, cut these into 112 trapezoids, measuring along cut edge at 2⅞" intervals.

You will need 56 of each of these:

2. Cut 1 strip 1½" wide into 4 "decapitated triangles", making cuts at 5¼".

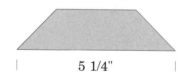

5 1/4"

Piecing and Assembly

1. Make 2 1/2 sets of the following strips:

Make 56 cuts at 1 1/2"

B   A

2. Make 56 of each of the trapezoid units that look like this:

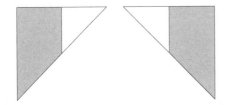

8. After the pieced border is applied, the quilt will measure 49" square.

9. Add a last border of any width desired.

3. Make 28 of each of the units that look like this:

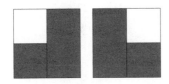

4. Make 24 of each of the following units:

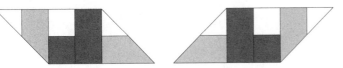

5. Make 4 corner units that look like this:

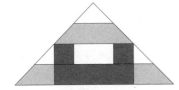

6. Make 4 border strips that look like this:

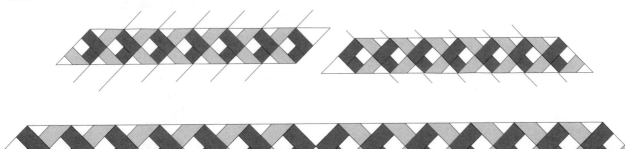

Sew one to each side of quilt.

7. Then add corners.

Border 9

After star is completed, add first border.

With 1" wide strips of border fabric, cut 2 strips 38½" long and sew to 2 opposite sides. Press.

Cut 2 strips 39½" long and sew to remaining sides. Press.

Fabric Requirements:

Fabric A (Background) - ⅔ yd.
Fabric B (Main) - ½ yd.

Cutting Instructions

Fabric A (Background)

1. Cut 4 strips 2⅜" wide. Cut into 56 squares 2⅜". Cut these diagonally to yield 112 half-square triangles.

2. Cut 6 strips 1½" wide.

Fabric B (Main)

1. Cut 2 strips 4¼" wide. Cut these into 14 squares 4¼". Cut these squares with an X to yield 56 quarter-square triangles.

2. Cut 3 strips 1½" wide.

Piecing and Assembly

1. Sew 3 sets of strips that look like this:

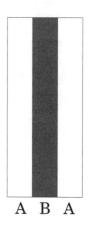

A B A

Cut every 2" into 56 segments.

2. Make 56 flying geese units that finish to look like this:

3. Make 56 arrows that finish to look like

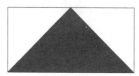

this:

4. Sew 4 border strips of 13 units each that look like this:

Sew two strips to opposite sides of quilt.

5. Add extra arrows onto ends of remaining border strips, following illustration. Sew onto quilt.

6. After the pieced border is applied, the quilt will measure 45" square.

7. Add a last border of any width desired.

In my quilt, I used scraps. Cut 1 dark square 4¼" with an X and you will get an arrow for each side. You will also need 4 rectangles 1½" by 2". The background is the same.

Border 10

After star is completed, add first border.

With 2½" wide strips of border fabric, cut 2 strips 38½" long and sew to 2 opposite sides. Press.

Cut 2 strips 42½" long and sew to remaining sides. Press.

Fabric Requirements:

Fabric A (Background) - ½ yd.
Fabric B (Main) - ½ yd.

Cutting Instructions

Fabric A (Background) and Fabric B (Main)

1. Place right sides together and cut 2" wide bias strips.

Piecing and Assembly

1. Sew bias strips of Fabrics A and B in pairs and press gently from the top, with seams towards dark.

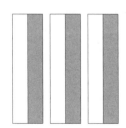

Sew 3 pairs together and press again.

Lining up ruler with 45° angle on a stitching line, make cuts at 2".

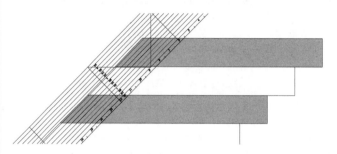

With cross line of ruler on cut edge, make cuts at each point.

Measure off cuts at 2".

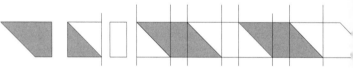

Cut 116 triangles.

These triangles should measure 2" raw edge to raw edge.

2. Make 4 border strips of 28 triangles , with 14 triangles going one way, and 14 the other way, that look like this:

3. Sew two border strips to opposite sides of quilt.

4. Add an additional triangle unit to each end of remaining border strips and add to quilt.

5. After the pieced border is applied, the quilt will measure 45" square.

6. Add a last border of any width desired.

Border 11

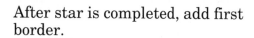

After star is completed, add first border.

With 2¾" wide strips of border fabric, cut 2 strips 38½" long and sew to 2 opposite sides. Press.

Cut 2 strips 43" long and sew to remaining sides. Press.

Fabric Requirements:

Fabric A (Background) - ⅝ yd.
Fabric B (Main) - ½ yd.
Fabric C (Accent) - ⅓ yd.

Cutting Instructions

Fabric A (Background)

1. Cut 4 strips 3⅜" wide. Cut into 42 squares 3⅜". Cut these with an X to yield 168 quarter-square triangles.

2. Cut 2 squares 3". Cut diagonally to yield 4 half-square triangles for corners.

Fabric B (Main)

1. Cut 4 strips 3½" wide. Cut into 44 squares 3½".

Fabric C (Accent)

1. Cut 5 strips 2" wide. Cut into 88 squares 2".

Piecing and Assembly

1. Make 80 units that look like this:

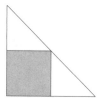

2. Make 32 units that look like this:

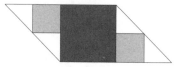

3. Make 4 units for right sides of border strips that look like this:

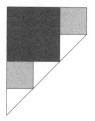

4. Make 4 units for left sides of border strips that look like this:

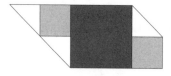

5. Make 4 corner units that look like this:

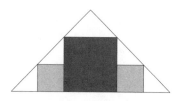

6. Sew 4 border strips of 8 units each, then add a right end unit and a left end unit.

Sew one border strip to each side of the quilt, stopping stitching ¼" from ends. Close up remaining seams.   Add corners.

7. After the pieced border is applied, the quilt will measure 51" square.

8. Add a last border of any width desired.

Border 12

After star is completed, add first border.

With 2½" wide strips of border fabric, cut 2 strips 38½" long and sew to 2 opposite sides. Press.

Cut 2 strips 42½" long and sew to remaining sides. Press.

Fabric Requirements:

Fabric A (Background) - ⅞ yd.
Fabric B (Main) - ⅜ yd.
Fabric C (Accent) - ½ yd.

Cutting Instructions

Fabric A (Background)

1. Cut 4 strips 2⅜" wide. Cut into 56 squares 2⅜". Cut diagonally to yield 112 half-square triangles.

2. Cut 1 strip 2" wide. Cut into 8 squares 2".

3. Set aside a ½ yd. piece to be sewn with Fabric C.

Fabric B (Main)

1. Cut 3 strips 3⅞" wide. Cut into 28 squares 3⅞". Cut diagonally to yield 56 half-square triangles.

Fabric C (Accent)

1. Set aside ½ yd. to sew with Fabric A.

Piecing and Assembly

1. With fabric A and fabric C right sides together, cut into 2" wide bias strips.

Sew strips into pairs and press gently towards dark. Join 3 pairs and press again.

Make a bias cut, lining up ruler with stitching line, and make cuts at 2".

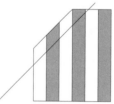

Cut at each point, lining up cross line of ruler with cut edge.

Then measure off 2". This should end at opposite point.

These triangles should measure 2" from raw edge to raw edge. Make 64 triangle units.

2. Sew a triangle onto each side of 56 triangle units.

3. Add large triangle of fabric B.

4. Make 4 corner units that look like this:

5. Sew 4 border strips with 14 units, reversing in the middle.

Sew two strips to opposite sides of quilt.

6. Add a corner unit onto remaining border strips. Add to quilt.

7. After the pieced border is applied, the quilt will measure 48" square.

8. Add a last border of any width desired.

Other Books by Trudie Hughes

Template-Free Quiltmaking

More Template-Free Quiltmaking

Even More

Template-Free Quilts and Borders

These books are published by:

That Patchwork Place, Inc.
P.O. Box 118
Bothell, Washington 98041

All of these books, as well as the Rotary Rule™ and Rotary Mate™, are available from:

Patched Works, Inc.
13330 Watertown Plank Road
Elm Grove, Wisconsin 53122
414-786-1523

Patched Works is a wonderful quilt shop in a western suburb of Milwaukee, Wisconsin. Here you will find 4,000 bolts of cottons for quilters, hundreds of books and patterns to excite you and quilts to view everywhere. Stop by sometime to visit.